BROKEN PIECES:

Nothing is Wasted

By

Ross Alan Hill

Broken Pieces

Published by Total Fusion Press

6475 Cherry Run Rd. Strasburg, OH 44680

www.totalfusionpress.com

ISBN - 10:0988370069

ISBN - 13:978-0-9883700-6-7

Cover Photos: Carl Shortt

Cover Art: Diana Smith

Editor: Andrea Long

Library of Congress Control Number: 2014935825

Published in Association with Total Fusion Press, Strasburg, OH. www.totalfusionpress.com

What are people saying about *Broken Pieces*?

"The supreme artist (God) uses broken things (like us) to make beautiful things for his glory. I appreciate Ross Hill and the way he opens our eyes to the elegant wonder of God's redeeming grace."
- **Dr. David Faust**, President, Cincinnati Christian University

"Through *Broken Pieces*, Ross Alan Hill captures divine encounters certain to leave readers amazed at life-changing experiences that have made a powerful difference in the lives of so many. Ross has done an exceptional job telling colorful real-life stories that make his book one readers won't want to put down."
- **Ray Sanders**, Chief Executive Officer, Water4, Inc. and Founder of GiANT Experiences

"'Fess up: we're all broken, battered people! Thus we all need the redeeming, reconciling touch of God through Jesus. In a deeply moving, transforming way, Ross Hill assures us: 'The God who is in Christ does make all things new.'"
- **Paul Mundey**, Senior Pastor, Frederick Church of the Brethren, Frederick, MD.

"The Story of Redemption...though old as time itself, Ross makes as fresh as today, making it applicable to all men and women. This book is the prime example that the Word of God never changes, but methods of presentation do... Jesus came to heal the brokenhearted, set the captive free, set at liberty them that are bruised...We are those vessels in the Potter's hand. He removes the flaws from some, repairs the brokenness of others, and for many gathers up the fragments, so that none will be lost to make us whole, to become a Redento Raffinato... May all that read this book know that they too can become redeemed elegance. To God be the Glory."

- **Dr. Herldleen Russell**, Supervisor Dept. of Women, Uganda East Africa Jurisdiction, Greater MD First Jurisdiction, Church of God in Christ, Intl.

"Ross Hill is simply a brilliant husband, father, friend, entrepreneur, and most importantly, child! *Broken Pieces* is about the art of life. How a loving, graceful, & tirelessly patient God can take the mess of our past & present, and turn it into the miracle of our future. Take a breath, relax, & enjoy the ride of falling in love with the greatest Father of all."

- **Clark Mitchell**, Founder - Senior Pastor, Journey Church- Norman, OK

"Within the words of this book colored by redemption, I am ever reminded that as a follower of Christ Jesus, He is the reason I am redeemed elegance. He made it all possible on a cross where He was broken by my sin. And yet He arose in redeemed elegance. Now I am to live on this planet as His breathing, living Redento Raffinato. Thanks, Ross, for this wonderful reminder of who I am, who made it all possible, and why I live."

- **Pastor Gary A. Jamar**, Morris Memorial Baptist Church, Ada, OK; President of Board of Directors for Malawi Orphan Ministries www.MalawiKids.com

"Ross is one of the most generous men I know — of his time, talents and treasures. This book is a vivid depiction of what it means to be a faithful steward of all God has entrusted to us, even the broken pieces. It will put you on a path to easily share your story and your faith. It will confront the reality that we aren't fine, but encourage you with the hope of Christ. Buy a copy for yourself and a case of them to give to everyone you know or meet in need. The manifestation of your purpose and potential truly is an inside out process."

- **Brian Hill**, CEO-Works24

"'Pick up the broken pieces and bring them to the Lord...' Jesus Christ is the only one who can restore you, re-create you, re-make you and renew you...into a masterpiece! My friend, Ross Hill, has captured this concept in a powerful way in *Broken Pieces*, a book that will inspire you to share your story of what the Lord has done. Your story can truly make a difference in many lives. Thank you, Ross, for obeying God and writing this inspirational book."

- **Randall Christy**, Founder, The Gospel Station Network, CEO-The Great Passion Play

"In a world of put-downs, Ross has given us beautiful stories of redeemed elegance. All of us have or will face times in our lives when we feel broken, vulnerable, and unworthy. The story of the vase reminds us that God can take our brokenness and make something beautiful. This book is full of hope!"
- **Anthony Jordan**, D. Min., Executive Director-Treasurer, Baptist General Convention of Oklahoma

"Through this powerful book, Ross puts the beauty of God's grace on full display. It is a story of redeemed elegance and radiant hope which brightly shines in our brokenness."
- **Peter Greer**, President and CEO-HOPE International, and author of *The Spiritual Danger of Doing Good*

"Broken? Shattered? In *Broken Pieces*, Ross Hill reminds us that as believers, we are all works of art; we are all redeemed elegance. Through many encounters, he illustrates that, 'It is the glory of God to take our brokenness and put us back together.' Ross knows of what he speaks. His own life and story is one of redeemed elegance."
- **Dr. David Wesley Whitlock**, President, Oklahoma Baptist University

"In his book, *Broken Pieces*, Ross Hill, who is an intercessor, evangelist, servant leader and a broken vessel, is an example of how God can deliver a person from his brokenness and remold him into a beautiful living vessel that God can use for His glory. Christ himself was broken, to make possible our salvation (Isaiah 53:3). He came to heal the brokenhearted (Luke 4:18). My friend Ross has written a book on HOPE; read it, enjoy it and give it away as a gift of HOPE. If God can use Ross, He can use you as well. Remember, 'One shall become a thousand'" (Isaiah 60:22).

- **Dr. Enrique Cepeda**, Executive Director, Thomas School of International Studies, Mid-America Christian University

"Broken Pieces is a must read for everyone who is yearning for God's great gifts of authentic HOPE and HEALING! Ross Hill is a mighty man of God who has written a book that I will recommend to all my friends and I encourage you to recommend to all your friends as well!"

- **Dr. Walt Kallestad**, Lead Pastor, Community Church of Joy, Phoenix, AZ

"I've known Ross Hill for many years as a top shelf banker, and this book is based on years of experience by a man who loves and cares for others. In reading this book, you will experience the heart of a man that lives out one of my favorite quotes by Nelson

Mandela, 'Our lives are borrowed. All we own is our faith and all we leave behind is our love.'"

- **Matthew Myers**, Co-Founder of GiANT Companies

"*Broken Pieces* illustrates God's intent to use individuals like Ross and even broken pieces of glass like Whatsit to speak into the lives of others God's plan of rescue and redemption. Ross, thank you for shining God's inspiring light on us."

- **Michael Brewer**, Attorney at Law and Founding Partner Hiltgen & Brewer, PC.

"Ross Hill introduced me to a piece of art that will forever have a place in my heart and home: Redento Raffinato. It is an exquisite vase with a shape that reaches for the sky. But the real beauty is in the story. God takes the broken pieces of our lives and molds them into a beautiful expression of his grace. Ross Hill gives this grace to everyone he meets. My Redento sits in a prominent place in my living room, and will forever remind me not only of God's grace, but my gracious friend Ross Hill."

- **Marty Grubbs,** Senior Pastor, Crossing Community Church, OKC. OK.

This book is dedicated to the One who redeemed me
from my brokenness.

"Declare his glory among the nations,
his marvelous deeds among all peoples."
– Psalm 96:3

ACKNOWLEDGEMENTS

To the love of my life - Raynell, you are a gift from God. Thanks for loving me, helping me and praying me through writing this book.

To my kids, I love watching you all have success.

To my parents, who loved me and taught me how to work.

To my grandmother Trudy, who planted the seeds of faith in my heart.

To my brother and his family, who would do anything for me and always has.

To my grandkids, who bring me joy every day.

To my friends and support team that have prayed for me as I wrote this book. Jim Stewart, Susan Stewart, Chris McGahan, Micah McGahan, Ray Sanders, Paul Foster, Carrie Foster, Tim Mills, Denise Mills, Ron Harris and Greg Gunn. Thanks for your support.

To my team that has advised me along this journey, playing the game we now call "Bob Goff": Jim and Susan Stewart, Chris and Micah McGahan, Ray Sanders, and of course, Raynell Hill.

To the Bank2 team, thanks for your support and encouragement. What a privilege to work with you.

To my editors, Randy Allsbury and Jennifer Gaidos – who helped a beginner get a great start.
BeyondYourManuscript.com

To my photographer, Carl Shortt - Wow, your photos are fantastic!

To my publisher, you went the extra mile to help me get this message of hope out to the world. Thank You!

CONTENTS

FOREWORD

Ross Hill is one of the most genuine and devoted followers of Christ I know. He doesn't need a pulpit to preach. He has used his platform as the CEO of Bank2 to impact thousands of lives, one at a time. I count it a privilege to call him friend.

Ross is a man of many talents, but I didn't know that writing was one of them until I read *Broken Pieces*. As a reader, I want writers to add value to my life. I want them to tell me something I don't know. I want them to challenge me to become everything God has created me to be. Ross has done that brilliantly.

I completely agree with Ross, "Everyone should have a Whatsit." And he will help you find yours. I have several Whatsits in my office. While I didn't call them by that name until reading *Broken Pieces*, that's what they are. And they have sparked some wonderful conversations. But that's just the beginning of this wonderful book. Ross has turned a piece of artwork, Redento Raffinato, into a metaphor that is larger than life. The stories he tells paint a picture of God doing what He does best—making something beautiful out of the broken pieces in our lives.

- **Mark Batterson**, *Author of* The Circle Maker *and Lead Pastor of National Community Church, Washington D.C.*

Chapter 1

WHATSIT

"The people were so amazed
that they asked each other, 'What is this?'"
– Mark 1:27a

Some years ago, I read in some book that everyone should have a **"Whatsit"** in his or her office. A "Whatsit" is a conversation starter, a one-of-its-kind or something so unusual that people are drawn to it so much that they can't help but ask, *What is it?* It is a **"Whatsit."**

I liked the idea, and for years I kept a railroad spike on my desk. It was very old, very rusted and small. Inevitably, people would ask me about it. Many times they would pick it up. I would tell them about being in the mountains of Colorado. We drove up to the top of a mountain pass to a tunnel that was dug for a narrow gauge train used back in the 1800s to take supplies to the west coast. The tunnel collapsed long ago, and I picked up the spike to remember seeing this remarkable part of American history.

I learned some of the history of the mountain pass, and discovered that 70-some brave Chinese men had lost their lives. They hung in baskets suspended by large ropes to place huge boulders on the side of the mountain so the railroad company could fill the area with dirt and make it flat and wide enough for the railroad tracks and trains. I actually drove our van across the section the Chinese laborers built over 100 years ago. I can still remember gripping the steering wheel so tightly that my knuckles turned white!

People were very interested in the story about my Whatsit railroad spike. It broke the ice and helped establish a relationship. Then we could move to the business matters, which brought them to my office. It was sort of like a warm-up band at a concert before the main act.

Back in 2009, I decided that I needed a **Spiritual "Whatsit"** in my office. I wanted an object that would be of great interest – like the railroad spike – but with a spiritual value. I wanted a Whatsit with beauty, something that would catch people's eyes and generate conversation.

About that time, my friend Chris McGahan and his son Micah were perfecting an idea that turned into a technique that turned into their signature that would set their artwork ablaze.

I am blessed to have Chris McGahan as a best friend. We love each other greatly. Most importantly he loves the Lord and is a great example to me of living your life for the Lord. I knew he was a believer the first time I met him. His faith was not hidden. Over the past 20 years, we have become great friends and I pray for him almost daily. Because of his faith and

2

our friendship, I have warned Chris that he is going to speak at my funeral whenever God takes me home. It would be an honor to have such a wonderful, God-fearing man speak for such an event. Without a doubt, Chris would honor God, and I know whatever he would say would be perfect. So what better guy could create my "Spiritual Whatsit" than Chris? (And Chris, I want my Redento Raffinato front and center at my funeral!) Not only are we the best of friends, but also, we are longtime friends, united together as brothers in Christ. I also happen to be his banker, and he named a pizza after me on the menu at Italian Jim's restaurant, The Ross Hill Super Pepperoni. Trust me: you have never, ever eaten a better pepperoni pizza. **I am serious!**

So, it was a natural thing for me to ask my friend Chris to use his art skills to make my "Spiritual Whatsit." Not only did he have to have the perfect item, it would be *one of a kind,* and I knew that he and Micah would pray over it as they made it. What could be better? I was so excited to see it and to see what God was going to do with it in my office. I was praying "Big, Bold and Audacious Prayers[1]," asking God to use it to His glory.

---

[1] Taken from *The Circle Maker* by Mark Batterson. Copyright © 2011 by Mark Batterson, Use by permission of Zondervan. www.zondervan.com

While I was praying, God was certainly guiding Chris and Micah. In fact, it might be best if Chris is the one to tell you how God was at work in his life.

Chapter 2

TRAJECTORY!

by Chris McGahan

"Jesus Christ the same yesterday and today and forever."
– Hebrews 13:8

"Trajectory. 1. The path followed by …an object
moving under the action of given forces."[2]

As I look at things in my life and paths that I have
taken, I like to look backward to see where these
things originated and where they have been. In the
ways that God has brought me, I have been able to
see a clear path or a trajectory in my life. I've learned
to consider and utilize that trajectory to confirm
present and future events as I move forward. If they
don't line up with the trajectory, then I ask myself, "Is
this the path for me?" I use it as one of the factors I
consider in determining the will of God in my life. I
think that a person can learn a lot by looking at his
God-directed   trajectory.

I have known Ross for about 20 years. When I first
met him and started to become acquainted with him, I
realized that he was a good man, a man who placed
God in an important place in his life. Over the years,
as we have grown closer, I can't help but notice the

---

[2] Definition retrieved from www.oxforddictionaries.com
Copyright 2014, Oxford University Press

trajectory that Ross's life has taken. I've watched him as he has grown closer and closer to God. I have seen him fine-tune his walk with God. It's amazing how our trajectories have intersected to God's glory!

Ross asked me to write this chapter about his Redento Raffinato vase that he aptly named, "God's Glory." He wanted me to write about the vase from my vantage point. Ross wanted me to expound upon the colors, the creation, the presentation of it to him and his wife Raynell, and even what occurred afterwards. It sounds like he wants to see a trajectory of his vase. I say "trajectory" because that vase, or more specifically, the story, it's meaning, and the purpose behind it is literally "on the move!"

It's a story that tells of God's redemption to the human race and God's grace in the process of making something beautiful and elegant out of people! At the time of this writing, this story of redemption through our blown glass has reached at least 118 different countries in the world. The story, as well as an actual Redento Raffinato, has even been presented to and received by a former Vice President of the United States of America!

The trajectory of the Redento Raffinato story began without fanfare about 26 or 27 years ago when I was at home watching television one day. I saw a Muranese Glassblower roll up some blue canes (canes are colored rods of glass stretched thin to about the size of a regular pencil) on a hot bubble of glass. He then blew the hot bubble until it was fairly large, and in the end of the process, opened the bowl up by spinning it quickly. When the centrifugal force caused the bowl to open wide, he quickly and skillfully swung the bowl upside down while it was connected to the pipe, and the glass bowl's edges folded like a big napkin. He gently nurtured the piece, making sure to maintain the artful folds in the bowl as the glass began to cool and stiffen. It took my breath away! I was amazed. I saw on the TV guide that the show was going to replay in a couple of days, so I set my VCR to record the show. Over the years, I would sit down and watch that show, and I loved it every time. Well, as things go, we moved a couple of times, and you know what that means – stuff gets packed away, and you can't remember where you stored various items. I spent several hours one week looking for that VHS tape to take to a video place to have it converted to a DVD. I never found that tape. I mentioned to my wife, Linda, that I had looked and looked and looked but couldn't find it. I was really disappointed! Oh well!

Then came my birthday. Linda remembered how much I loved that video, and the idea came to her to see if anybody in the area gave glassblowing lessons. She found a place about 35 minutes from our house, and she signed me up for a series of lessons. The lessons were all day Saturday and a half of a day on Sunday. She gave those lessons to me as my birthday present. Wow! The thought of me actually blowing glass had NEVER even entered my mind! I was so excited that I could hardly contain my enthusiasm. I found myself counting down the days until the lessons started.

Finally, the day of my first lesson arrived. On my drive there, I was thinking about my new endeavor. I was thinking I might want to do a lot of this. I was pretty tied up with our restaurant business and didn't really have much, if any, spare time. As I was driving down the road in my pickup, I just prayed out loud, "God, what do you think about me doing this glass blowing stuff? Would you have a problem with me pursuing this?" Of course, I heard no audible answer, and I sat there just thinking about what I had just asked. Then I remembered something from the Word of God. (The number one way that God speaks to His people is through His Word. If you haven't taken the time to hide God's Word in your heart, you're going to have a difficult time hearing from God!) I remembered that when Moses, under God's direction, was going to build a tabernacle in the wilderness, God gave Moses instructions. God spoke to Moses concerning the man who was to oversee much of the construction. God said, "*(3)...and I have filled him with the Spirit of God, with wisdom, with understanding, with knowledge and with all kinds of skills— (4) to make artistic designs for work in gold, silver and bronze, (5) to cut and set stones, to work in wood, and to engage in all kinds of crafts*" (Exodus 31:3-5).

8

Wow! It was then that I realized that God would anoint men to build things and create things of beauty and works of art! I knew that God is the same yesterday, today, and forever (Hebrews 13:8) and that if He would anoint someone under an old covenant to create works of art, He would do it today under the new covenant.

Encouraged by these thoughts, I prayed a very simple prayer. I said, "Lord, I ask you to anoint me to understand glass and how to manipulate it to create things of beauty. If you will do that, I will do my best to glorify You with it. I ask you to help me make works of beauty that will bless people." I enjoyed the lessons so much that I signed up for another series. I was completely hooked. Over time, I began thinking how nice it would be not to have to drive thirty-five to forty minutes to blow glass and that if I had my own furnace, glory hole, and annealer, I could speed up the learning process. It takes a long time to gain proficiency in blowing glass. To become proficient, you have to break a lot of glass! Can you begin to see the trajectory of where this is all going?

Fast-forward to 2009. My son Micah and I had been working in our fledgling studio in my backyard for about 4 or 5 years. We had just started making our Redento Raffinato vases a few months earlier and had enlisted the help of a new friend, who just happened to be one of the top glassblowers in the world, to help us make our Redento Raffinatos bigger and refine our

9

technique. Janusz (pronounced Ya-Noosh) Poźniak is his name, and he agreed to come down to help us make some 30-inch tall Redento Raffinatos. By this time, the Lord had begun to reveal to me some metaphors in the making of our Redento Raffinatos as it related to a life lived in Christ, and I began to tell folks about it. Once again, can you see a trajectory, or a progression of events in motion?

The new concept of our Redento Raffinato, as I remember it, was first received, affirmed, and recognized, by my good friend, Ross Hill. When Ross heard about the Redento Raffinato and the story behind what it symbolized, he said, "I want one!" He told us that he wanted it to be predominately red, symbolizing the blood of Christ. He wanted the body wrap (the thin line of glass horizontally encircling the piece from top to bottom) to be white, symbolizing the righteousness of God. He also wanted some black in it, symbolizing the sin that was dealt with and overcome by the blood of Jesus. He also wanted multi-colors in it, symbolizing all the people of the world.

I remember thinking that I liked the colors that Ross picked out and what they symbolized. I also remember being excited because Ross's Redento Raffinato was the first one commissioned because of its spiritual significance. I look back now at how it all started and see a clear path, or trajectory, of events that God has been using to bring us to the calling he has in our lives to proclaim his message of redemption through what we do in glass.

Emboldened by the trajectory we were on, and being assured that God was in this process, we began Ross's piece with a sense of divine purpose. I asked God to help us bring it to completion and to allow it to be a blessing to Ross. With Janusz overseeing and helping us, we went through each step until it was done. It was beautiful. It had all the colors Ross said that he wanted in it. We made a few more Redento Raffinato vases, each one with their own unique color combinations. When they were all finished, I called Ross and told him that his was ready and that we actually made several so that he could take his pick.

He and his wife, Raynell, showed up at our house and came into our backyard. We lined the vases up on a counter and told him to pick which one he wanted. He quickly picked the one we made for him over the other ones. I was really excited! This was a big deal to Micah and me. Before Ross arrived, we had everything in the backyard looking awesome. I was playing some appropriate music that I thought fit the occasion and had the Redento Raffinatos all lined up on a granite tabletop by our grill.

As I mentioned earlier, Ross was instantly drawn to the one we blew especially for him. When I presented it to him, he said he felt something go through him. I could tell he was emotionally touched. As I remember it, he even got a little teary-eyed and seriously exclaimed that he definitely did feel something! He was amazed. He wasn't expecting to feel anything! Ross said he wanted to name it, "God's Glory" and put it in a very prominent place in his office. I remember thinking, "Wow, he's serious about this!" I was a little surprised at everything that had just happened as it related to how Ross reacted – in a good way, of course! I'm sure that every artist wants his work to be received well, and we were certainly excited to see Ross and Raynell so excited. It kind of made our day! Little did I realize the trajectory we were all on at the time.

To learn more about Chris & Micah McGahan, visit their website www.BellaForteGlass.com.

Chapter 3

WHY THE REDENTO RAFFINATO?

"...I have loved you with an everlasting love;
I have drawn you with unfailing kindness."
— Jeremiah 31:3b

You now know that my "Spiritual Whatsit" is my very own Redento Raffinato. You heard from my friend Chris, but there's a bit more that I would like to add in regards to how I knew that Chris's creation was the perfect item to serve as my "Whatsit."

One of the things that Chris and Micah learned in the creation of the Redento was that they had to stick the broken pieces back into the fire more often. Once they began to form an object, they also learned that they had to work on the *inside* of the Redento before they could be concerned about the outside. Chris says, "This is exactly what God has to do with us. He first starts working on our hearts to get it right."

Once they perfected the process, they started blowing a few pieces and putting them on display. Chris did some research to come up with a perfect name for their newfound art technique. He found two Italian words to describe their new creations: **Redento Raffinato,** meaning **redeemed elegance**, two perfect Italian words to describe their new art creation. They sold like hot cakes. They could not keep them on the shelves! To this day, the Redentos are their number one selling item.

When I saw the Redento in Chris's restaurant, I instantly knew I had found my "Whatsit." I commissioned the Redento, which is now prominently displayed in my office. Many of my guests ask me about my beautiful vase. This gives me the opportunity to tell them about how the one true and living God can deliver them from their brokenness and remold them into beautiful, living, breathing human Redento Raffinatos.

And so, on September 30, 2009, sometime between 5-6:00 p.m., my wife, Raynell, and I drove over to the Bella Forte Glass Studio after work. I was excited to go see what my buddies had created for me. I knew it was going to be special. I almost felt like a kid on Christmas Eve waiting for Christmas morning. I could hardly wait for work to end. It seemed like I hit every red light on the way over to his studio, taking forever to drive the less than seven miles there.

Earlier in the day, Chris had called to tell me that he had several Redentos for me to choose from. He wanted me to know that if I did not like the one he had blown, per my order, I could choose from one of the others. I remember walking into the outdoor area where Chris had several Redentos displayed. He told me to pick the one I liked. I made a bee-line directly to the special Redento Chris had blown for *me*. It was easy to pick out and was more beautiful than I could have hoped.

It was very tall, 33 inches to be exact. It was shaped rather like a tear drop but with a long and graceful neck. One side of the opening at the top was much higher than the other. I looked it over; **it was everything I wanted and more.** It was full of multiple colors to represent all of the people of the world. It had rough, sharp and jagged black lines crisscrossing the entire vase to signify our pain, our loneliness, our sin, our separation from God. It was bathed in red to signify being washed in the blood of Jesus and contained a thin white line to signify being made pure and whole and complete. Somehow, they were able to start the white in the base and stretch it all the way to the pentacle of the vase.

I told Chris that I loved it. He picked it up and held it up in the sunshine. The sun was now lowering in the western sky, and the sun's rays lit the vase up like neon. **Spectacular!**

Chris handed it to me. I cradled it almost like a baby in my arms. As soon as I did, I started tingling all over, a warm feeling, similar to goose bumps or the hair on the back of your neck standing up. **It felt great!** I did not know what was going on, and I turned quickly and handed the vase to my wife. Remember: the vase is 33 inches tall, and Raynell is only 59 1/2 inches tall (in her heels).

I said, "Do you feel it? Do you feel the tingling?"

Raynell said, "No."

I couldn't believe it. I kept asking her, "Can you feel it?" I asked Chris about the tingling I felt.

Raynell said, "I wouldn't feel it. The vase is not mine; it is yours."

And Chris said, "It is a sign from the Lord that your vase is going to be used to glorify Him."

All the way home, Raynell and I talked about what happened when Chris handed the Redento to me. It was **an amazing moment that I pray I never forget.** I believe God was confirming to me that He was pleased with my "Spiritual Whatsit." I believed He was saying that He was going to use this vase and my office to bring inspiration, healing and redemption to my guests.

Why a Redento Raffinato? Honestly, I did not really know at the time. I just thought it was cool, and I loved the symbolism. However, in the past few years, God has revealed to me that many of the nearly 1,400 people who have walked through my office door are broken. I truly had no idea, but they are hurting deep down in the innermost part of their souls. I, too, have known this kind of pain firsthand. Something we gloss over is that **God knows the pain too,** and He knows it firsthand. His son Jesus died a brutal death on a cross for a crime He did NOT commit. He endured the pain, the hurt, the rejection, the loneliness and the agony so that we could be redeemed. **It is the Glory of God to take our brokenness and put us back together,** to give us a hope for tomorrow and make us more beautiful than when we first began.

Chapter 4

FOUR YEARS AGO

"Even in darkness light dawns for the upright,
for those who are gracious and compassionate and righteous."
- Psalm 112:4

I will remember September 30, 2009, as a special day for the rest of my life. It was a beautiful Oklahoma fall day. The sun was bright, the sky was blue, and the wind was calm. It was a perfect day to pick up my Redento Raffinato. The following day, October 1, 2009, I placed it on display in my office.

I recently retrieved my prayer journal from September and October of 2009 and read what I was praying about when I ordered the Redento. I read what I prayed about the day I picked it up and read what I prayed about the day I put it in my office. In fact, I read about what was going on in my life for the 30 days preceding my ordering the Redento through the 30 days after putting it in my office. It was fun reliving those days through my prayer journal.

One thing that struck me as I read was that I was a man on a mission. I knew exactly what I wanted. I knew the colors I wanted in the Redento. I carefully explained the details to the artist, and I told him what each element was to represent. The idea was as clear as a bright sunny day, and Chris immediately understood what I wanted when I described it to him.

Interestingly, I recorded in my prayer journal my thoughts upon seeing and holding the vase for the first time. Even though I am now 60+ years old, my memory of those events is completely accurate. Obviously, this was an amazing, life-changing and defining moment in my life.

My good friend Pat Snyder, a very accomplished artist, was in the bank the first week I had the Redento on display. I recorded part of our conversation in my prayer journal. Pat marveled at the beauty of the Redento, and she told me that she understood why I had such a warm tingling feeling when Chris handed it to me. She said that it was a sign from God, which was basically the same thing both Raynell and Chris had stated.

One of the things I prayed about four years ago was that I would have the opportunity to use the Redento to tell *everyone* that comes into my office the story of redemption. I had asked God to let me use it to share the story with **thousands of people**. I can honestly tell you that I have shared the story with everyone that has come into my office except for three people. I am constantly reminded about failing to share the story with those individuals. I wonder why I failed. I wonder about their stories. I wonder how badly they needed to hear the Redento story. I worry about their souls. It reminds me that **I must not let it happen**

again. I must be faithful to do what I promised the Lord I would do.

A bit of research revealed that in the four years I have owned the vase, 1,400 people have heard the Redento Raffinato (redeemed elegance) story in my office. I promised God that I would share the story with everyone who enters my office. I have shared the story with every new employee we have hired, every customer, every service guy or gal. I have shared the story with congressmen and governors, with CEOs and doctors, and with Federal Reserve Bank and State Banking Department examiners. Literally, people from all walks of life have heard the story of the Redento. Recently I even shared the story with a customer who was VERY angry. After hearing the story, he calmed down, and when he left the bank, he shook my hand and we wished each other well.

Of those **1,400 people,** I have prayed for 781 of them before they left. My office has turned into a huge platform for the Lord. God is answering prayers that were uttered four years ago. It even appears that He is answering the prayers at an increasingly rapid pace. Amazingly, people are now calling me and asking for appointments to bring family members or friends by my office to see the Redento and hear the story. I never imagined any of these things happening when I commissioned my vase.

When I unearthed these figures, I stood in awe of what has been happening in my office. You see, when I started the bank, we dedicated it to the Lord. My buddy Chris (the artist) came out and anointed the doors of the bank, my office doors and the board room doors. We have started each board meeting for the past 12+ years with prayer. We pray before each loan committee and management meeting. We pray over each open position, and when we hire someone, I personally pray with each new employee.

The Redento is a natural outgrowth of the culture we have put into place at Bank2. Does that mean we are perfect? Does that mean that we don't have problems? Does that mean we don't have to let people go? **NO!** But it does mean that we attempt to put God on the throne and **let Him run our business.** It means that when we make a mistake, we own up to it. It means that we conduct business with character. It means that we sometimes have to say we are sorry. It means that I must apologize if I have wronged someone.

The Redento is a daily reminder that I am saved by grace. It reminds me of my brokenness and that, without the love and forgiveness of God, I would be nothing but a bunch of broken pieces headed for the city dump. Many days as I look at the Redento, I think about how I screwed up my life and the lives of people I love. It helps me to realize that except by the love and mercy of God Himself, I would be bound for the scrap pile too. The Redento helps me to remember how great His love is. It also helps me to remember there are a ton of people that desperately need the Lord. They need His forgiveness, and they need to allow His loving grace and mercy to invade their hearts. This is what motivates me to share the story. I put the Redento in my office on October 1, 2009. It is interesting to note that it only took me four days to give the vase a new name. On October 5, 2009, just four days after I picked it up at the glass studio, I changed the name from **Redento Raffinato** to **God's Glory**. Why? As I remembered and confirmed through reading my prayer journal, I changed the name because I felt **God's Glory** was a better fit. To me, it is what happens when we surrender our lives to Him. He re-melts us. He reshapes us. He remolds us into something more beautiful than the original. **This, my friend, can only happen with GOD –** *"God's   Glory."*

The Redento is simply symbolic of what Jesus wants to do for all of us. All we have to do is ask Him. The vase has no power in and of itself. The power is in the Lord and His great love for us. The power is in understanding that no matter where you are in life, no matter what you have done and how many times you have done it, no matter the sin, no matter how many times your life has been broken or how many pieces your life has been broken into, God loves you and will forgive you. The power of His redemption is in the blood of Jesus.

"(1) I lift up my eyes to the mountains— where does my help come from? (2) My help comes from the Lord, the Maker of heaven and earth." - Psalm 121:1-2

Chapter 5

EVERYBODY HAS A STORY

"… put your hope in the Lord,
for with the Lord is unfailing love
and with him is full redemption."
- Psalm 130:7

The past four years have provided me with a fresh insight into mankind. Of course I knew that people hurt and become discouraged. I just did not realize the extent and depth of the pain that lives just under the surface. I did not understand that everyone has a story. When I placed my Redento Raffinato in my office and started using it to tell people about Jesus, I began to comprehend just how banged up and bruised the people of this world are. I began to understand why God put it on my heart to commission this phenomenal piece of art I call "God's Glory." My discovery has made for some very uncomfortable moments in my office. The flow of tears has caused me to keep a healthy supply of tissues in my office. People truly are hurting.

Of the 1,400+ individuals who have walked into my office over the past four years, I can tell you that most have been deeply hurt and still suffer from the pain. Frequently, they know the Lord, yet they too suffer from pain. Countless stories center on being broken. Unfortunately, many have been broken for a long time before they enter my office. The most normal-looking people in the world enter my office, only to have God, through the story of the Redento, help to unmask the pain with which they are consumed. Many of them finally discover that, in spite of their broken condition, God loves them with an everlasting love.

On most occasions, the conversation begins in a normal way. Seldom do my visitors show their pain because we have all learned to hide it. Sometimes they don't even realize that they are in desperate need of a life saver, or that they need to be redeemed. I have learned that the "normal look" is only skin deep.

Unfortunately, I think most people are hurting. They are sick, they need help, and they want help but are afraid to feel any more pain. They have buried it in an attempt to stop hurting. At best it is a thin façade.

Clark Mitchell, Pastor of Journey Church in Norman, OK, recently said, "Being Broken is painful. If you are not willing to live through the pain of brokenness, you will never live a life of restoration. You have to live through the pain of brokenness to get to the blessings of restoration." He went on to say, "Brokenness will lead to more brokenness or to more blessings." I believe Clark is correct.

"And we know that in all things God works for the good of those who love him, who have been called according to his purpose." - Romans 8:28

Let's be honest. We all struggle with discouragement from time to time. It can be overwhelming. It can be painful, very painful. Sometimes the discouragement comes in a flash with no warning whatsoever. It just blindsides you. A friend of mine worked for over a year on a mission trip. He prayed about it without ceasing, he helped to plan the trip, he trained workers for the trip, he raised money for the trip, he saw himself being used in this foreign land to reach the lost for the Lord. He, along with the rest of the team, filed for their visas for the trip, and everyone received a visa except him. He waited and waited and finally started making inquiries about his visa. He discovered that his visa was being held up due to concerns about the validity of his current passport. The hour came for the team to leave, and he still did not have his visa. He was discouraged.

We all live with some discouragement. Some face struggles with their bosses, some with personal finances, some with sickness and disease. It could be most anything. As I write these words, my great friends Jim and Susan are spending yet another night in the hospital with their adopted son. He has had three kidney transplant surgeries and numerous other health problems that have affected his entire 25 years of life. I know it has to be difficult on all of them. I know it must feel like they know everyone working at the hospital on a first-name basis. They have prayed that Marquise's health would be completely restored so many times they could not possibly count the number of times they have done so. It is tremendously discouraging to see their son in pain, in the hospital, with life-threating issues. We were at church when they received a text from Marquise, stating that he was going to the emergency room. Discouragement can overtake you anytime, anyplace.

And how discouraged would you feel if you were Marquise? He must be asking, *"Will this ever end? Will I ever be healthy?"* Who can answer except the Lord?

While they have all been dealing with these health issues for Marquise's entire life and at times it seems like it will never end. They all realize God is in control and they put their trust in him.

My mom, now 89, sits at home by herself. Most of her friends are gone. She is losing her memory, and even reading a book has become almost impossible for her. Watching TV is problematic too. She is lonely and bored, and each day seems to last an eternity. She is decidedly discouraged by her current lifestyle. She did not see it coming to an end like this. She has been a very social person with tons of friends her entire life. Now her friends are immobile and have lost their health too. Most are gone or will soon be gone. Life can be hard, lonely, and discouraging as a senior citizen.

I have noticed in some instances once a person is significantly discouraged, it just keeps coming, like ocean waves rolling to shore 24/7. Sometimes it feels like the waves will never stop. They just keep coming and coming. It makes it hard to catch a breath or find dry land.

The Bible is full of stories of men and women who loved the Lord and suffered from discouragement too. Sometimes God moved almost instantly to remove the problem, but more often, the discouragement lasted far longer, sometimes for extended periods of time.

Before I put the Redento in my office, I thought most everyone was fine. Now I know people are not fine. Many need help. Americans don't like pain, so we take more pain medicine than any other country in the world. When the pain meds don't work, we drink to cover it up or we buy something else to hide the pain. We do all kinds of negative things to conceal the pain or to keep from facing the pain. But the One who can remove the pain is waiting on us to seek Him and use His power to be conquerors (Revelation 12:11).

I am beginning to believe that one of the ways Satan has been able to deceive us is by convincing us that when we are broken we are not good enough for the Lord. He could not possibly forgive us, so we must hang on to our brokenness and live with it daily. We walk around defeated. We look good on the outside, but we are totally broken on the inside. We become weak because we carry such a heavy load. As a result, we spend money we don't have, thinking that we can buy our way out of the pain. Satan laughs all the way to the bank. He has destroyed our witness and has defeated us. We have become ineffective Christians. We are defeated by our sinful past because we hang on to it instead of letting it go; thus, we snuff out the power of God in our lives. We destroy our witness.

Honestly, **discouragement is part of life. God uses these times to build character, to deepen our faith, and to prove that He is Lord.** Sometimes we are called to a life that is going to be discouraging. I instantly think of Job, Jeremiah, and Ezekiel as prime examples. Even so, we must see that God used their life experiences, disappointments and circumstances in glorious ways for His purposes. To deny those facts would be to overlook key factual realities from the Scriptures. Realizing these points doesn't make it less painful or difficult, but by faith we realize that He is preparing us.

We *must* recognize that we were created for His purpose and that we are to be obedient to Him. We also need to remember that this time will pass and until it does, God is with us. I recently heard Max Lucado preach and promote his new book, *You'll Get through This.* He said, "We need to call on Him and His promises to help us overcome. We need to remember what was *'intended for evil God turns to good[3].'"*

The next time you become discouraged, the next time you want to quit, the next time you think you cannot take another step, remember these words of Isaiah: *"(1) But now, this is what the Lord says— he who created you, Jacob, he who formed you, Israel: 'Do not fear, for I have redeemed you; I have summoned you by name; you are mine. (2) When you pass through the waters, I will be with you; and when you pass through the rivers, they will not sweep over you. When you walk through the fire, you will not be burned; the flames will not set you ablaze. (3) For I am the Lord your God, the Holy One of Israel, your Savior...'"* (Isaiah 43:1-3).

Listen, the truth is that when we are broken, God can remold us, remake us, and re-tweak us. It is in the midst of our brokenness, in the trials of our pain and hurt, and in the wake of defeat that the Glory of God is manifested. It is at such times that the world can see He redeems us. It is when we are broken that we realize we cannot do this thing called life without Him. When we are broken, the pain is acute, and many of us attempt to mask it. We just keep hurting, and we hurt those around us. It comes out in all kinds

---

[3] "We need to call on Him and His promises to help us overcome. We need to remember what was *'intended for evil God turns to good"* Max Lucado, YOU'LL GET THROUGH THIS, Thomas Nelson, Inc. Nashville, TN 2013

of negative ways, but when we turn to God and realize that *"God is our refuge and strength, an ever-present help in trouble"* (Psalm 46:1), we begin to understand how great He is. As the Scriptures teach, *"The Lord Almighty is with us..."* (Psalm 46:7a).

The truth is in the fact that He helped us overcome. The power is in showing the world that, through Christ, we overcame. Even though we all have a story, our stories do not end in defeat and insignificance or under a mask. Our stories are stories of victory, of overcoming our problems and disappointments, of overcoming our pain and heartaches through the power of Jesus alive in us. If we believe in Him, we have been forgiven. Regardless of what our stories may be, we can be forgiven and can inherit the gift of eternal life.

Each of us has a story that needs to be shared with the world.

The following stories in this book are just a sample of the stories that have come through my office. I could write many, many more. Undoubtedly some I don't even know. I don't need to know them. The Lord has directed their steps to my office. My role is to be an obedient storyteller. The vast majority of the time, I don't know much about the people sitting before me. I don't know their personal lives, their needs, their loneliness, their emptiness or brokenness. As I tell the Redento story, their lives collide with His love, His mercy and His grace. The healing power of redemption is released at that moment. The Holy Spirit's role is to move and convict or heal their hearts. Redemption comes from the Lord.

Chapter 6

SONJA ROSE

"May the God of hope fill you with all joy and peace
as you trust in Him, so that you may overflow with hope
by the power of the Holy Spirit."
– Romans 15:13

Most of my visits with people in my office are about business. People generally come to see me to discuss the possibilities of the bank loaning them money for their businesses, or they want the bank to do business with them in some form or fashion. Sometimes they want us to make a donation to some social project in which they are involved. Seldom do I know many details about their personal lives. In other words, I don't know what they are going through at home with their spouses, their children, or their parents. I don't know about their health. I don't know the challenges or problems they are facing. But as in anything, there are exceptions. In some situations, I know that people are hurting. I know some of the details, and **I know why they are broken.** I think it is easier to not know.

A few years ago, a friend of mine, Sonja, was engaged to be married. She worked in the health care industry. Months before her wedding, she started having some health issues. Because she knew how to conduct the exam and had access to the equipment, she performed her own exam, and the results **took her breath away.**

She went to see a doctor, and he confirmed her exam results. She had breast cancer and needed to have immediate surgery – **a mastectomy.**

She was very young, in her early 30s, and her world was suddenly falling apart. Every dream she had was crushed. Every hope for the future disappeared. Her plans were ruined. Fear gripped her to the innermost part of her soul. She was dismayed. I believe she was in a place greatly feared by most women and a place that perhaps most of us can never fully comprehend.

Her inner pain was almost unbearable, and those who loved her and cared for her watched in unbelief. Sometimes, **life throws things at us that just should not be.**

Sonja's fiancé loved her and stood by her and still wanted to marry her. She had family and friends and a church that prayed over her. She had one really special, loving, good friend. Denise was kind of a big sister or maybe even a second mother due to the difference in their ages. Denise stood with Sonja and prayed over her for hours and hours during the days, weeks, and even months that followed. Many times, this God-given friend went to her chemo treatments with her just to love on her, just to be there for her, just to share the load.

Sonja and her fiancé decided to get married before her treatments started. Kind friends put a wedding together in just a day or two. Sonja and her husband were married and enjoyed a short honeymoon before her surgery.

Sometime after the surgery, and just after her chemo treatments started, Sonja was at the bank for a meeting. I wanted to talk to her, but I was scared. All kinds of excuses went through my head. What could I possibly tell her that would encourage her? We were friends, but we were not "close friends." What if I said the wrong things? What if I made it worse? What does a guy know about such things? The more I thought about it, the more I felt like I should *not* say anything. Somehow, I was able to fight through all of the negative thoughts going on in my brain. I believe the Holy Spirit kept encouraging me in spite of my doubt. I asked her to step into my office. Clumsily, I made small talk for a minute, and then I pointed out my Redento Raffinato. I explained the meaning to her, and I told her I believed God would take her brokenness and remake her into a beautiful **Redento Raffinato** (redeemed elegance). I told her that I had been praying for her and that I was not going to stop praying for her.

Honestly, the conversation was very difficult for me. The words were really hard for me to come by. I was on uncharted ground. Awkward would be putting it mildly. Remember, Raynell and I had a friendship with this young lady, but **we were not extremely close**. Here I was – a healthy man, much older, trying to give a young female hope for a better day. Are you kidding me? Thankfully, the Holy Spirit controlled the conversation. As Sonja sat in my office with a scarf covering her hairless head, very thin from the trauma her body had been going through because of the cancer, the surgery, and the chemo, God used the moment to provide encouragement to her and to motivate me to do even more. What she was going through was taking its toll. Even now, as I type these words, my eyes fill with tears just remembering her brokenness. She thanked me for visiting with her and for telling her the Redento story. We prayed before she left my office.

I was hurting for her. **I felt almost powerless to help her, and I hated that feeling almost as much as I hated the cancer and what it was doing in her life.** That night, as my wife and I drove home, we decided that we needed to do more. We decided to have a Redento blown for her. We told the artist the story, commissioned the piece, and Chris and Linda McGahan went to work on a very special item. They put the most beautiful colors of green, pink, and white into the vase. Linda named the vase **"Sonja Rose,"** a double-entendre. The name for the hand-blown art perfectly described a beautiful delicate rose in color and style. The name also conveyed the meaning that God would raise Sonja up over her health issues. We then asked our mutual friend Denise, the friend that had been praying for Sonja perhaps more than any other person in the world, the friend who was like a sister or a second mom, going to some of Sonja's chemo treatments and providing emotional and spiritual strength, to take **"Sonja Rose"** to Sonja at her next chemo treatment. We wanted the art to provide hope and a promise for new and better days. We wanted it to be given to her in the middle of the difficult chemo treatments as a sign from God, that **He was with her and she would get through it.**

As Sonja began to heal, she wanted us all to visit the Bella Forte Glass Studio to observe Chris and Micah blowing a Redento. One evening, we all gathered at the studio, and Sonja and her husband heard firsthand from the artists the true meaning of the Redento Raffinato. **God restores the inside first.** She took tons of photos, asked lots of questions, and at one point even participated in helping blow the Redento.

Today, Sonja and her husband live a wonderful life. She writes a blog and often speaks about her life experiences and how God breathed life back into her soul. Her life is full of hope and promises. She has contemplated writing a book. She uses photography to express her love for the Lord. Sonja is a walking, breathing **Redento Raffinato.** Truly, through the love and mercy of the Lord, she is redeemed elegance.

"Be strong and take heart, all you who hope in the Lord."
- Psalm 31:24

Chapter 7

COREY

"'...For I know the plans I have for you,' declares the Lord,
'plans to prosper you and not to harm you,
plans to give you hope and a future.'"
- Jeremiah 29:11

I was never blessed to meet Corey in person. He is the son of a friend of mine. I understand that, to many, Corey was an average teenager or young man. But from what I have learned about Corey, I think he was one special guy.

Corey loved football. He played football for Piedmont High School in Piedmont, OK. Having raised three young men who played sports, I can tell you that they all dream of being part of a record-breaking team. Corey was no different, and in his senior year of high school, his team had a record-breaking season! They *lost every game*, which was not exactly the kind of record-breaking season one dreams of, especially as a senior. At 17, Corey had already learned more about life than many three times his age. He told his mom, "If you can stay together as a team when you are losing, then you are really a team." He also told her that, "many teams find it hard to stay together when they are winning, but it is really hard to stay together when you are losing. With each new game, you are confronted with self-doubt that you will never win." He may not have won the games his senior year, but he definitely figured out that there is way more to life than winning a football game.

After graduating from Piedmont High, he enrolled at University of Central Oklahoma in Edmond, OK. One summer evening between his freshman and sophomore years, a few weeks before school was to start, Corey's life ended way too soon. He was involved in a tragic car wreck involving excessive speed and bad tire or two.

Corey's mom, Beth Parrett, had to bury her 19-year-old son. It broke her heart and the hearts of others in the family. Beth was lost in grief as any mom would be. She had a new job calling on bankers. Unfortunately, she was emotionally drained, depressed, and physically exhausted. She hurt so much that she could hardly bear to see another customer. In Beth's words, *"It was just a very hard, crappy day."* So she went to Starbucks to buy a cup of coffee in the hopes that she would then be able to muster enough courage to make one more customer visit. It would be to see me at Bank2.

As she pulled up to Starbucks, she saw a homeless man. She got out of her car with some trash in her hand, and the man walked up to her and took the trash out of her hand and held the door for her to go inside. It was a bit uncomfortable for her.

While Beth sat in Starbucks trying to work through her depression, she kept watching the homeless man. He was holding the door as people entered and sometimes even opened the car doors of people carrying multiple drinks.

Beth said, "It seemed to make the guy happy just to serve people." She asked the cashier if he came there often.

The reply was, *"Every day."*

Beth said, "I want to buy him a gift card, but I want to be sure he will use it to buy food and drinks at Starbucks."

She was assured that he would use the card for that purpose, so she bought him a $25 or $30 gift card, gave it to him, and got in her car to drive over to Bank2.

As she was leaving the parking lot, Beth saw the homeless guy standing in a chair outside Starbucks with his hand raised high, waiving at Beth to say, *thank you.*

Beth later said, *"It was the first time my heart had smiled in a long time."*

When Beth showed up in my office, we started talking. I sensed something was wrong with her. I had no knowledge of Corey's death just months earlier. She seemed distant and hurting, but seemed as though she had something on her mind that she needed to say. I awkwardly asked her if she was OK. She said she saw a sign driving over to see me that said **Jeremiah 29:11** and wondered what the verse said. I opened my Bible and read it to her. *"'...For I know the plans I have for you,' declares the Lord, 'plans to prosper you and not to harm you, plans to give you hope and a future.'"* Beth later told me that was one of her happiest moments.

About that time, I told her the story of my Redento Raffinato. Beth kept looking at my vase as I told her how it was blown from scraps of broken pieces of glass, from other items the artist tried to blow, that had fallen to the floor and broke into hundreds of pieces. As I told the story, Beth never stopped looking at the vase. Tears were streaming, and she went through a ton of tissues. After I finished explaining how the vase is a perfect example of what God can do with someone's life when that life is surrendered to Him, Beth began to tell me about Corey. The pain and hurt lodged deep inside my friend's heart was excruciatingly painful. It was very difficult for me to hear her story. Beth said, *"I felt just like all those broken pieces."* She wanted to be thrown into the trash too. But then she said, *"If God could put all of those little pieces back together and form this beautiful vase out of all of that brokenness, maybe He would do that for me."* **God** used the vase and the Redento Raffinato story to **breathe life and hope back into Beth's soul.**

Beth has since realized that God orchestrated that entire day – the homeless guy at Starbucks, the sign that read **Jeremiah 29:11**, the fact she was calling on me, and that I not only had my Bible, but also had the verse highlighted and was able to read it to her and share the story of how God is a **God of Redemption**, and then there was my prayer for her, asking God to put her broken pieces back together. All of these encounters combined started her healing process.

Today, Beth and her family miss Corey deeply, but God has moved and brought healing. As a result of a list of goals Corey had written a few months before his death, one being that he wanted to give back to Piedmont and the football program, the family formed the Corey Hammett Memorial Scholarship Foundation. Thus far, the Foundation has awarded five scholarships. You can find more information on Facebook by searching the name *Corey Hammett Memorial Scholarship Foundation*.

One of the other things Corey wrote was that he wanted his legacy to be that he gave back to people in need. While Beth and her family were at the hospital that horrible night she kept saying, "Something good is going to come out of all this tragedy."

It is my understanding the young man driving the car

that night was one of Corey's best friends. Corey knew Jeff had some issues but Corey loved him just the same. Corey told his mom that Jeff had an alcohol problem and he needed someone to care for him. Corey decided that someone was him. Corey didn't quit the football team and he didn't quit on his friends either. Corey was living out his legacy.

Corey and two others lost their lives in the wreck, but Jeff survived. The "something good is going to come out of all tragedy" is that Jeff's life has completely changed. He no longer drinks; he is married and lives a productive life. He and his wife had a son recently and they named him after his best friend, the guy that never gave up on him...**Corey.**

Beth told me that to this day she has a pink post-it on her desk of something I said to her that afternoon in my office. She said it gives her comfort and that she recently shared it with a co-worker because his wife was facing huge health challenges. She hoped it would encourage him as it has her. Her pink sticky says, **"Everybody has a story."**

Chapter 8

DR. BENNY PRASAD

"We wait in hope for the Lord; he is our help and our shield."
- Psalm 33:20

Do you know Dr. Benny Prasad? He is a musician, song writer, singer, preacher and **record world traveler.** Yesterday, Benny was in my office telling me his story. Several years ago, the Lord put on his heart the task of taking the Gospel to all nations. You may be familiar with the verse, *"Therefore go and make disciples of all nations, baptizing them in the name of the Father and of the Son and of the Holy Spirit..."* (Matthew 28:19). Well, Benny felt that God was personally challenging him to take this verse to heart and go into *all* of the world.

Benny took the message so seriously that he set out to visit every country in the world, not as a tourist, but as a man called by God to **share the message of Jesus.** Benny has hundreds and hundreds of stories about his travels. He actually showed me his passports. The stack is about four inches high. He also showed me a certificate which certifies that **Benny holds the world record** for visiting every country in the world in the fastest time frame.

He told me the story of needing and wanting to go to **one last country** to complete his journey of visiting every nation in the world. The one last country he needed to visit was Pakistan, but because relations between Pakistan and India are not good, when he attempted to get a visa, he was told **NO!** He was discouraged by the government official in Pakistan who said that there were only two ways for him to get a visa to visit Pakistan. He either had to have a blood relative living in Pakistan or he had to be invited by the Pakistani government. The official basically said it was a lost cause; Benny would never get a visa.

Benny was not going to be denied. He spent the next four days making **334 phone calls,** exhausting every avenue he could think of to get into Pakistan, but no one could help him. Benny was praying to God, "Why would you open all of these doors around the world and not open this last door?"

Sometime later, he was in North Korea, staying in a 43-story hotel. Benny was getting off of the elevator to go to his room on the 32nd floor. Two men were getting on the elevator as Benny was getting off. Benny overheard the two men speaking in Hindu, and he asked the men where they were from. They said that they were part of an Official Delegation from Pakistan. Benny quickly told them his story of trying to get to all 246 countries in the world. He explained that **Pakistan was the last country on his list** and that he was not able to get a visa to visit Pakistan. He asked if they could help him.

The men told Benny to come to their room at 10 p.m. They gave him their room number, which **was on the 32nd floor, right across the hall from Benny!** He could hardly believe it, and he thanked God and waited and prayed until 10 p.m.

At 10 p.m. Benny walked across the hall with his guitar in hand and played and sang a song for the two men. Benny said, *"The presence of the Lord was in the room. The Holy Spirit immediately moved in the men's hearts."* One of the men said he was the **Speaker of the Pakistan Parliament**. He told Benny not to worry about getting a visa; he would personally take care of it.

Benny got his visa, and guess what else? **The visa was signed by the man that told him he would never get a visa!** Don't ever give up on God. He directs our steps.

Benny says that he learned that, *"God is not only the God of the righteous but even a person that is trying to do evil at some point must yield to God's will."*

But wait, there is even more to his story.

Benny was the firstborn in his family; thus, much was expected of him. However, Benny had many health issues. He was born with severe asthma and with 60% of his lungs damaged. He had to take heavy doses of steroids, which caused him to develop rheumatoid arthritis. His immune system was significantly weakened to the point that his life is threatened daily even to this day. **His body was broken.**

He was expected to follow in his father's footsteps. His dad was a highly-regarded scientist in India. Benny needed to excel in the same fields. Benny was not able to live up to the dreams and expectations of his family. He brought shame and disappointment to his family. **His mind, in a fashion, was broken.**

Benny grew depressed, and the pressure and stress became unbearable. He contemplated suicide at the age of 16. **His emotions were broken.**

Then Benny's mom stepped in and convinced him to attend a youth retreat. There began his journey towards a new life. He moved from being the shame of his family to being their pride. God's power brought the most powerful change in Benny's life. Benny met the Lord, and God spoke to him, saying, *"Benny, even though you have been called USELESS ALL YOUR LIFE, I NEED YOU NOW, AND I CAN TRANSFORM YOUR LIFE AND MAKE YOU A NEW CREATION."*

Benny says, *"If I could be made useful, anyone in this world can."* What a remarkable story.

As I shared my Redento story with Benny, I realized that Benny is a living, breathing Redento Raffinato.

Benny said, *"Remember, you are never too bad or sinful for God to redeem and transform."* Benny is living proof. **God can create redeemed elegance out of anybody.** What road blocks are you dealing with? What pain are you living with? What delivers pain to the innermost part of your soul? Whatever makes you feel broken, like scraps destined for the dump, remember that God is ready to redeem you and transform your life into something far more beautiful than the life you started with. He is faithful to His promises. Turn your life over to Him and allow Him to redeem you.

To learn more about Benny, visit his website at www.bennyprasad.com.

Chapter 9

A LOVE THAT NEVER LETS GO

"He heals the brokenhearted and binds up their wounds."
– Psalm 147:3

Earlier this year, my buddy Derek called and asked to meet me for lunch. It had been several months since we had been together, so I was excited to see him. Derek is a fantastic filmmaker. He owns a company named Lampstand Media and has won many, many awards for his work, including an **Emmy!** We met at our normal BBQ restaurant and spent some amount of time catching up on all of the things that had happened since we last saw each other. We were having a great time.

Derek brought his iPad, and I thought he was going to show me some pictures of his little girl or a clip from his most recent film. **I was right.** After lunch, he reached for his iPad and turned it on as he said, *"I have a surprise for you."*

I began watching an amazing film. It was shot in the Bella Forte Glass Blowing Studio in Edmond, OK. I recognized my friend's studio instantly. Derek was intensely watching me as I watched the video, and he had a huge grin on his face that seemed to go from one ear to the other. The film featured a lady speaking and the artist, Chris McGahan, blowing a Redento

Raffinato. Derek said to me, *"Do you recognize her?"* and then a few seconds later, before I could even respond, he said, *"Listen to what she is saying!"* Of course I was watching and listening. Derek's huge smile had now changed to a bit of a frown as he said again, *"Look at her; listen to what she is saying! Don't you recognize her?!"* My friend was a little frustrated and surprised.

After I finished listening and watching the film, my friend told me the rest of the story. Derek said, *"Remember, her husband called you and asked for an appointment. He was working for a charity down the street from the bank. He came to see you last summer, and he brought his wife with him. You shared the story of your Redento with them."* I was starting to remember but still struggling a bit.

When they came to see me, the wife was suffering from a disorder called **cutting.** Cutting is a form of self-injury; the person literally makes small cuts on his or her body, usually on the arms and legs. Somehow it helps them to control their emotional pain. When the husband called me for the appointment, I thought about saying **NO** because I knew he was coming to ask for a donation for the non-profit he worked for. I am so thankful I said **YES.** He never mentioned that he was bringing his wife to our meeting, nor did I know she was suffering. When he showed up, he apologized about bringing his wife to the meeting. However, I am inclusive by nature, so the more the merrier for me. We discussed the purpose of his coming, and when he had concluded, I turned everyone's attention to my Redento Raffinato and told the story of my beautiful vase.

I explained how it was hand-blown by my friend and went on to explain how it was made from **broken pieces of glass,** leftover from other art pieces that he had attempted to blow but had fallen off the blow pipe and onto the floor, shattering into hundreds of pieces. I explained how I had asked the artist to put as **many colors** as he could into the vase to represent all of the people of the world; **black** to represent our troubles, our discouragement, our sin, our separation from God; **red** to symbolize being washed in the blood; and **white** to symbolize being made pure and whole. I told my new friends, *"This is a perfect image of what happens to an individual when you completely surrender your life to the Lord. He picks up all of your broken pieces and remolds them and remakes you into something more beautiful than you were in the beginning."*

Many times, when I tell people the story, I get an immediate response. Sometimes, I don't get any response. In this case, I got what I would term a "positive response." The couple divulged some personal information. He explained that he was a pastor but had been fired by his church. He was working for a charity while they recovered from the emotional pain of being fired. He really did not elaborate a lot. I could tell there was much more to their story, but I did not pry. I gave them a copy of the book *The Circle Maker*, and I asked if I could pray for them before they left. They said, *"Yes, we appreciate your prayers."*

Honestly, I don't remember thinking about them again. Then Derek showed me the video of a lady talking about **her brokenness** and how she felt like **scraps that needed to be thrown away**. Derek told me that while they were preparing to shoot this film, she said something like, *"Do you know **a banker named Ross Hill?** He has a vase like this in his office."*

Chris said, *"He is my banker, and I blew his Redento."*

She said, *"He shared the story with me and my husband and God used his story and the Redento to give me hope. I think that was the moment God started my healing process."*

I remember leaning back in the booth as Derek finished his story. I was speechless, and I had tears in my eyes. Eighteen months earlier, I just did what I always do the first time someone comes into my office. I shared the story of redemption by using my Redento Raffinato. I promised the Lord I would tell every person that comes into my office. I promised my wife I would do so. I had no idea how God used the story, my office, the Redento to **give this lady hope**. I had no idea it was her first step in her long healing process. I was just trying to be obedient to what I had promised God.

Some 18 months later, God used my friends Derek and Chris to help this lady tell her story of redemption to the world. God is so amazing. **God directs our steps**. He uses us, and many times we don't have any idea that we are being used. What a blessing it was to find out that God had used me to help this couple. We don't get or deserve any praise. To Him be all the glory – only **HIM!**

Visit my website to see and hear the story, www.RossAlanHill.com.

Chapter 10

I DON'T KNOW WHY I AM HERE

"A person's steps are directed by the Lord."
– Proverbs 20:24a

Warren came into my office barely able to walk under the heavy load he carried. He looked like one of those weight lifting guys we have all seen on TV, competing to be the weight lifting champion of the world. Warren could have been wearing one of those back support braces you see on the competitors and employees of Wal-Mart and Sam's Club. But he needed way more than back support. You could see the pain on his face, in his steps, in his demeanor. He kept saying, *"Why am I here? Why am I in a banker's office? Why did my friend send me to a banker?"*

I sure didn't know either. All I knew was what I had learned from a text I received at 6:57 a.m. from a mutual friend. She wrote, *"Would you be able to visit with a man I know who is suddenly blind-sided by life?"* What kind of a question is this, sent to me by a lady I have only just met a few weeks ago?

I was perplexed and wanted to say, **NO!** I sure wanted to know more before I agreed. I wanted to say, *"My schedule is totally full, maybe another time."* I looked at my calendar and saw one unscheduled hour in my entire day from 1-2:00 p.m. I needed that time to return calls, read emails, and just to breathe. Besides, I am a CEO of a bank! Does this have anything to do with banking? But **something in my gut was saying I needed to see this guy.** I wrote these words back to my friend, *"I think so, about 1:00 p.m.?"*

The next thing I knew, it was 1:00 p.m., and Warren was in my office. He was so labored by the emotional pain he was feeling that he could barely speak. I believe it literally hurt for him to talk. Warren is no small guy. He works outside with his hands. He is fit and about 6 feet tall. Because the pain was almost unbearable, Warren was struggling to hold back the tears. It made talking to a complete stranger even more difficult and uncomfortable – uncomfortable for both of us. His confusion about being in a banker's office seemed to add to the difficulty.

I told him that I did not know why he was in my office but that we would figure it out together. I gave him time to breathe and let it out. The words came slowly and painfully, almost one word at a time. Bit by bit, the story came out, but honestly, his hurt was deep and it was so excruciatingly painful for him to tell me his story. Gradually it came out, and about halfway through he said again, *"Why am I here, in a CEO's office?"*

This time I told him I knew why he was here.

He quickly said, *"WHY!?"*

I told him I would explain in a minute, but to, "*Go ahead and finish your story. I think you need to get the weight off your shoulders.*"

It was very hard for me to hear his painful story. Honestly, I did not want to hear it, but this guy needed somebody to listen and to care. At this point, God wanted that somebody to be me. I rearranged my schedule to get thirty more minutes with Warren.

When Warren finished his story, I motioned to my vase and told Warren the Redento Raffinato story. I told Warren the entire story, every detail, and I compared the broken pieces of the vase to his broken life. I told him there was nothing right about what had happened to him. **Nothing!** But God was with him. God would help him pick up his life. I told Warren that he would come through this and that his life would get better. I told him that I knew he felt like the broken pieces of glass lying under my vase. I knew he wanted to be thrown away forever so the pain would stop. I explained to Warren that one day **God would breathe life back into his soul.**

I told him of God's promise, "'*...For I know the plans I have for you,' declares the Lord, 'plans to prosper you and not to harm you, plans to give you hope and a future...'*" (Jeremiah 29:11).

I also reminded him of Job's story and words, *"Though He slay me, yet will I hope in Him..."* (Job 13:15a).

Near the end of our meeting, Warren looked at me and said, *"I know why I'm in a* banker's *office."* I gave Warren a book and shared one more scripture with him. I prayed for him and offered to get him some professional help. I encouraged him to take the help. I asked him to call me the next day. He said he would. I hugged him and shook his hand as he left.

As I walked to my next meeting, I said, *"*Lord, I am a banker, *not a counselor, but thank you for using me and my Redento to give Warren hope."* On the way up to the 6th floor, I prayed for Warren.

As I was driving home, I was reflecting on the day and how God directed Warren to my office. Apparently, through no real planning on my part, my office has become a place of healing, even for complete strangers. I never envisioned my office being used for such purposes. How did this happen? Should it be happening? Do I have time for this activity? I tossed this over and over in my mind. I am not a counselor. I don't feel called to be a counselor. I don't want to be a counselor. But, **I do want to obey God. I want to use my office and life as a tool to spread His Word and His Love.**

God used the Redento Raffinato vase to give Warren hope and encouragement. I was able to use the Word to provide hope and a future. I was able to use my position to give him hope. I was able to use my connections to get him professional help.

My friend, Dr. Enrique Cepeda, reminds me all of the time that we need to be *willing, available,* and *obedient.* He says that some of us are *willing* but not *available.* Some of us are *available* but not *willing.* Some of us are simply not *obedient.* But Dr. Cepeda says, *"God can use us in powerful, radical ways if we will be willing, available and obedient."* Enrique says, *"God will give us divine appointments that are many times totally out of the ordinary."*

Even though I did not want to have the meeting with Warren, even though I felt woefully inadequate to help him, and even though I was totally covered up, I decided to be *willing, available* and *obedient.* God did the rest. I am praising God that I made the correct decision. I also pray that I will make the right decision the next time.

Chapter 11

DIVINE TIMING

"In their hearts humans plan their course,
but the Lord establishes their steps."
– Proverbs 16:9

Most of us believe in divine appointments and have heard that "timing is everything." I prefer to call it *"Divine Timing."* To me, *divine timing* is when God lines everything up to happen in His time. I would like to tell you about one such occurrence my pastor and I experienced firsthand.

I attend Crossings Community Church in Oklahoma City. Our pastor is Marty Grubbs. Marty is a very good guy. You would like him instantly. Under his leadership our church has grown in size beyond even his own imagination. Thousands of lives have been changed for eternity. Our church has a global outreach. Without question, God's hand is on Marty Grubbs and his ministry.

Early last year Marty and I tried to get together a number of times. We were somewhat successful, and I always enjoyed our lunches. Each time we would schedule a lunch, I asked him to swing by the bank. I wanted to show him the bank and, more importantly, my office. Like many of us, Marty's schedule is overloaded, and it just seemed to never work out. We would have lunch, but he never found the extra time to stop by the bank. Finally, we agreed that even if I had to bring lunch into the bank, Marty was coming to my office. Interestingly, Marty never asked me what the big deal was about coming to my office. I guess he just assumed that most CEOs want to show off their business or office. In this case, I had something special that I wanted to show Marty.

Early last year, well before Easter, Marty came to my office. We had a great meeting, and of course, I shared my Redento Raffinato vase with Marty. It was fun to watch him as I told him the story. As I proceeded to tell him how the vase was hand-blown from **scraps that were destined for the trash and the dump,** Marty got up out of his chair and took an even closer look at the vase. He wanted to know more about it. He asked me a bunch of questions, including how he could reach the artist. Marty wanted a Redento blown for himself. I provided Chris McGahan's name and number and the location of his art studio in downtown Edmond, OK. Marty was like a man on a mission.

I believe Marty called Chris from his car to schedule a meeting as he was driving away from the bank. He met with Chris and commissioned him to blow a Redento. Marty asked if he could bring a camera crew to film the process of creating his Redento. Then, on a glorious Easter Sunday in 2012, Marty preached five or six times that morning to about 12,000 people. His sermon was about **redemption**. The music was the perfect accompaniment for both the day and the message. During the sermon, a video was shown of Chris blowing Marty's Redento. When the video was over and the lights were out, several spotlights were directed to illuminate Marty's **46-inch Redento Raffinato standing tall, center stage.**

A story of redemption was illustrated throughout the service in music, prayers, sermons, and an amazing video. The video highlighted the broken pieces of glass, destined to be thrown away, saved by an artist with an idea. The artist was able to save the fragments and blow them into a **redeemed elegance vase,** shining in all of its glory. *It's a perfect image of what our Creator wants to do in each person's life –* **a story of hope, played out dramatically at Crossings on Easter Sunday 2012.**

Recently, Marty and I spent some time discussing the vase and that Easter Sunday morning. Easter and Christmas may be the most difficult Sundays to preach. So often, pastors are looking for something fresh and bold and memorable for two reasons: **One,** everybody in attendance knows the basic story. **Two,** many won't be back until the next major holiday. For these reasons, a pastor feels pressure to try hard to reach the congregation with something that will stand out in their minds. Marty called the Redento, "**a game changer.**" Marty has said that he knows that **people have not forgotten the service.**

Looking back on the course of events, I know God was orchestrating **"Divine Timing"** for Marty to see the Redento in my office. Marty was thinking about Easter Sunday months before Easter. He was praying for a great message, a way to illustrate Easter in a fresh way. Marty had no idea that God would lead him to a bank CEO's office to find unique artwork to amplify the meaning of Easter. God's Word says, *"In their hearts humans plan their course, but the Lord establishes their steps"* (Proverbs 16:9). I know God ordered our steps so that Marty would see the **Redento Raffinato** at the perfect time and so that God could put it on Marty's heart to use the Redento Raffinato on Easter Sunday 2012. Using more of Marty's words, *"It was perfect timing."*

Chapter 12

DIVINE LOCATIONS

"Lord, I know that people's lives are not their own;
it is not for them to direct their steps."
- Jeremiah 10:23

We've talked about divine appointments and divine timing, but have you heard of *Divine Locations*? A couple of years ago, my wife and I were purchasing some life insurance, which required me to have a medical exam. The insurance company wanted to send a medical technician to my office to perform the exam. You know, measure my pulse, blood pressure, blood, urine...how embarrassing! I have a very public office with a ton of glass in the walls. I did NOT want the tech to come to *my office*. I wanted to go to *his office*. I tried and tried to move the meeting location to the medical tech's office. Nothing I tried worked. The company insisted that their tech must come to my office. I was not happy. Little did I realize that God was orchestrating a *divine appointment* at a *divine location*.

When the tech showed up, I tried to be nice to him. I explained that I hated to do all of these things in my office and the restroom of the bank. He assured me that he could be discrete. He was a likable man and about my age. We carried on a friendly conversation between the administration of the various tests and his peppering me with what seemed like a hundred health questions.

As we concluded our meeting, I pointed to my vase and told him it was hand-blown by a great friend and customer of the bank. He was intrigued and thought the vase was "outstanding!" I told him the vase was called a Redento Raffinato, an Italian phrase meaning *redeemed elegance*. I went on to explain to him that the vase was blown from broken pieces of glass from other works of art that fell off of the artist's blow pipe, onto the floor and broke into hundreds of pieces. The artist picked up the broken pieces, the scraps of junk that were destined for the dump, re-melted the broken pieces, reformed them, and blew them into this wonderful vase. I went on to share that this is exactly what God does with each life when we surrender to Him. He picks up our broken pieces and re-melts them, reforms them over and over into a magnificent piece of art, more beautiful than the original.

As I turned my head from the vase to look into the eyes of my new friend, tears were streaming from his eyes. He began to tell me that he works as a medical tech through the week and a part-time pastor on the weekends in a small rural Oklahoma church. He and his wife had been married for 26 years. He came home about three months ago to find his wife waiting for him. Her bags were packed, she handed him some papers and said, *"I am divorcing you."* She walked out, never to return. He said he was devastated. He said it came out of left field and that he had no idea she was leaving him. Then he went on to tell me that this coming Sunday was to be his last Sunday as the pastor of the church.

I asked him why, saying, *"Did the church ask you to resign?"*

He said, *"No, I am resigning because I am a failure."*

We talked a bit more as he tried to get his composure back. He told me that the church had been great to him and did not want him to quit. He said, *"It is too painful. I have failed. How could I be a pastor?"*

I asked him to give all of this pain, suffering, and shame to God. He could pick up the broken pieces of his heart and life and re-mold them into something more beautiful and useful than they had ever been.

We prayed together in my office. We hugged each other, and he said that he was going home to contact the board to ask if Sunday could be his first Sunday as a re-molded pastor.

God used my insurance physical exam as a *divine appointment.* He used my office as a **divine location,** and he used my Redento Raffinato as a *divine instrument* to help this man feel redeemed, lift a burden from his shoulders, and become re-molded as a man and a pastor.

No matter how much I tried to move the meeting to the medical tech's office, God had other plans, and His plans always happen. **Praise God! He directs our steps.**

Chapter 13

CASA DE LA REDENCION

(Spanish for **House of the Redeemed**)

*"The Lord is close to the brokenhearted
and saves those who are crushed in spirit."*
– Psalm 34:18

In July of 2013, I was asked to speak in Dallas for the CEO Institute. My good friend Chris McGahan and I traveled to Dallas and had lunch with another great friend of mine, Tod Bush. Tod runs the Red Dot 100x program for his family-owned business, Red Dot Buildings in Athens, Texas.

We had a great time at lunch. Chris and Tod hit it off. I love introducing my friends to each other and watching God create new friendships. While we were visiting, I asked Chris to play one of his videos about his Redento Raffinato art. Tod watched intently and asked numerous questions after seeing the video. In fact, he made some preliminary plans to visit Chris and have dinner in his studio in Edmond, OK. He was thinking about bringing his wife up from Dallas to have dinner and have Chris blow something for her while eating the world-famous Ross Hill Super Pepperoni Pizza!

It is amazing how God used this introduction to **spark an idea**. A few days later, Ray Sanders called me using FaceTime. His wife, Stephanie, and Tod's wife, Robyn, are involved in a ministry to women in Honduras. They have created a safe house for battered and abused women and are using the house to restore these ladies. Not only do they provide a safe place for them, but also, they teach them about the Lord. While their primary goal is to disciple the women, their secondary goal is to help them receive an education. They want the women to graduate from high school and eventually college. They want them to have employable knowledge and skills. Stephanie and Robyn hope that one or more of these women will become entrepreneurs.

The purpose of Ray's FaceTime call was to show me a Skype call between Robyn in Texas, Stephanie in Oklahoma, and the ladies in the safe house in Honduras.

They were showing the ladies in Honduras the same Redento video that Chris had shown Tod a few days earlier in Dallas. Apparently, Tod showed the video to Robyn. Robyn and Stephanie talked and decided it was a perfect video to show the ladies they care for in Honduras. The video conveys such a strong story of how God takes our brokenness and puts the broken pieces of our lives back together. It is a story of *hope*. Robyn and Stephanie believed the video would give hope to these ladies in the midst of their brokenness. The ladies in Honduras don't speak English, so Robyn and Stephanie asked their partner, Androlla, to translate what Chris was saying on the video. It was fun watching it all take place *live* on my phone! Amazing! Robyn and Stephanie have decided to name their safe house *Casa de la Redencion* or *Redento House*!

God orchestrated this entire chain of events! None of this was planned by any of us, but **it was planned** by the Lord. That is the way God works. He directs our steps. If Chris had not gone to Dallas with me, he would not have met Tod. If Chris did not show Tod the Redento video, Tod would not have suggested it to Robyn and Stephanie. If Robyn, Stephanie, and Androlla had not shown it to the ladies, they would not have been blessed by the video's message of the hope of being redeemed.

God directs our steps.

Back in 2011, I was preparing to go to China for the first time. Our group had a planning meeting at the bank, and one of my friends going on the trip, Lance Humphries, encouraged me to take some photos of my office, featuring my Redento Raffinato. Lance believed that the Chinese business leaders would really identify with the vase and the story behind it. He believed they would enjoy seeing an American bank CEO's office and would be amazed by the story of my vase and how I use it in my office. I took some photos and used them in my PowerPoint on both of my trips to China. Lance was right. He had a great idea.

Months later, I was able to share my Redento Raffinato in person with various Chinese business leaders in my office. These were men and women who I had met on my trip(s) to China. The impact of seeing my Redento Raffinato in photos was, as Lance predicted, very profound. They wanted to visit my office and see my Redento and hear the story in person. They also wanted their photo taken with me and the Redento. **The power of the vase is the story of God's redemption.** The Chinese business leaders get it. In fact, I was able to take a couple of them to dinner to watch Chris and Micah blow a Redento. One of the Chinese business leaders asked Micah to come to China and start a glass-blowing business. He wants him to blow Redentos. He thinks many, many Christian Chinese business leaders will want to buy them for their offices.

God used these stories to give me an idea.

I asked Chris for permission to have the videos translated into Chinese and Spanish so that we could use the video in various countries now and have them available for future mission trips. Since that time, many other friends have offered to have them translated into other languages such as Portuguese and French. My friend Derek Watson who shot the two videos has agreed to redo them when the translations are completed. In fact, some of the translations are being done as I write these words. Before the end of 2014, I believe the two videos will have been translated into the primary languages of the world and will be used to convey hope and redemption through Jesus.

Nine years ago, my friend Chris prayed and asked God to use his art to bring glory to Him. He promised God that he would use his art ability to His glory. To this day, Chris wants people to see God in his art. From humble beginnings, taking lessons, renting time in a studio, and then to an outdoor area in his backyard, and finally to a modern studio, God is answering Chris's prayers. I believe it is accurate to say that God has used the artistic gifts He gave to Chris in ways well beyond what Chris had ever imagined. His art is being used to give hope to the broken, not only in downtown Edmond, OK, and Oklahoma City, but **around the world.**

And Jesus said, *"Go into all the world and preach the gospel to all creation"* (Mark 16:15).

Only God knew how the seed He planted in the life of Chris McGahan would take root. God's Word says, *"Before I formed you in the womb, I knew you."* God knew that in just nine years Chris's art would circle the globe, proclaiming that Jesus is Lord, that Jesus and Jesus alone can redeem the broken pieces of our lives.

Chapter 14

REDEEMED ELEGANCE

"God is our refuge and strength,
an ever-present help in trouble."
– Psalm 46:1

Bank2 is located in a seven-story office building in Oklahoma City. We share the building with multiple tenants. One of the first tenants I met back in 2001, just before we opened Bank2, was a husband and wife team, John and Pat, who own and run a small business specializing in Federal Government contracting.

John is the CEO and President and a retired USAF Major jet pilot – a really good one. Not only was John a great pilot, but also, he is really smart as evidenced by his beautiful bride, Pat.

Pat is Vice President of the company. She is the first person to greet every guest that enters the door of their business. Her welcome is always warm and inviting. To talk to Pat is to instantly respect her. Pat's beauty is enhanced by her outstanding professional dress and the love she shows for her husband of 54 years.

These two are, without a doubt, in love. You would be blessed to know them and see how they love the

Lord, their kids and grandkids, and their forty employees. They love life.

We quickly became friends. We always share casual conversations as we pass in the halls and in the elevators or parking lot. Pat and John are just sweet people. Trust me, **you would like them.** They are hardworking and don't know when to quit. In fact, John just celebrated his 83rd birthday last week.

In the midst of what should have been their "golden years," Pat was diagnosed with a malignant parotid tumor (salivary gland tumor), which required three surgeries, including facial reconstruction (facial sling). It was devastating news for Pat. As Pat said, the *"Physician of all physicians..."* (our Precious Lord and Savior) *"...assembled a medical dream team"* to solve her health problems. They performed these surgeries over a two-year period with no infection, no rejections, no long-term discomfort, no side effects, and no medications – simply the power of prayer at work. We all prayed for her, and we all felt for her. Some five years later, Pat is a cancer survivor. She comes to work every day. Her facial features are a bit different now, but Pat has not changed, except that she is stronger in her faith and singing His praises even more. Pat says that she is *"a living testimony of the power of prayer,"* the prayer of her family, friends and church.

One day when Pat had returned to work after her surgeries, I heard her voice out in the receptionist area. I was standing near my Redento Raffinato in my office and all of the sudden, I raised my voice and yelled, *"PAT, PAT, come in here!"* (My mom taught me to never yell to a person in another room, especially a lady. Sorry, Mom!) As I said her name a third time, I quickly walked through my doorway to greet her. I shook her hand and asked her to come into my office. I told her that I had something new I wanted to show to her. She and I walked into my office and over to my vase. Pat noticed the beauty of the vase instantly. As we stood together admiring the work of art, I told Pat the complete Redento Raffinato story. I explained to her that it was hand-blown from scraps of glass the artist was throwing away. This time, instead of throwing the broken pieces away, the artist decided to try to make something out of the fragments. He hand-picked some scraps from the discarded junk and positioned them perfectly. He then stuck them back into the fiery furnace, reaching temperatures of 2000 degrees, so that he could re-melt the pieces and begin to reform them. He had to stick the broken pieces back into the glory hole many times, but slowly and perfectly, the artist started blowing life back into the brokenness. When he was done, he had created this beautiful work of art. I said, *"Pat, this is just what God has done with your life. You are just like this beautiful vase. Once, you turned every man's head in this building. I have personally witnessed it for several years. Today, Pat, you continue to turn every man's head, but now, instead of just seeing your outer shell, they see your heart.* **Pat, you have never been more beautiful!** *Once people only saw the outside shell; now* **everyone** *sees the beauty of Christ living through you. Before all of this happened to you, some people knew you were a Christian based upon what you said. Today, they* know *you follow Jesus because they can see Him when they look at you."*

With those comments, Pat and I hugged each other in my office and wiped a few tears away. Pat asked if she could bring John down to see the vase and hear the Redento story. I said, *"Of course. Bring anyone you like."* I think Pat has brought many of her employees down, and she has brought her kids in to see the Redento and hear the story. She has even stopped by with some of her vendors.

The entire time this conversation was taking place it was as if I was watching from across the room. I never had any intention of sharing those words with Pat. I had never even thought about Pat in relationship to my Redento. The Holy Spirit took control when I heard Pat's voice. I know everything I said was inspired by Him to bless her. It blessed Pat for me to tell her what I saw and felt. It blessed me to share the story with her. But these were not "feel good words." **NO!** These were inspired words spoken in love and in truth to a friend I admire.

Honestly, it has not been easy for Pat to come to work, to walk into the building, to see her friends, to see her employees, to see her customers. I am sure it has been hard to see her kids and grandkids. I am sure it is hard to look into the mirror or at photos. I cannot imagine the pain she feels. But to this day, she is sweeter than ever. She is a joy to be around. She never has a frown, she never complains, she never says she is having a bad day. Pat put on the Armor of God and set forth on the journey. She does not feel sorry for herself. She is a fantastic example of a child of the King, trusting His plans, living by faith, letting Him direct her steps. **Pat is a Redento Raffinato, a living, breathing, walking example of what God can do with a life fully surrendered to Him.**

Chapter 15

BROKEN VIOLINS

"Your wound is as deep as the sea.
Who can heal you?"
– Lamentations 2:13b

In October 2013, Kyle Dillingham came to visit with me about a concert we were planning. Kyle is an extremely talented violinist, singer, and song writer. You must take the time to hear him in person if you ever have the opportunity! This was our first real meeting. We had only briefly spoken at the recent Water4 Gala. Kyle was the featured entertainment for the event. I was excited to have Kyle come to the bank to discuss our upcoming event.

We spent a good deal of time getting to know each other. I like to think we became instant friends. After I shared my Redento Raffinato with him and the story and meaning behind my vase, he asked me if he could run out to his car and get something he needed to share with me. He came walking back into my office with a large brown cardboard box full of violins, not just any violins, but dirty, dusty, worn out and **BROKEN** violins. As Kyle grabbed one out of the box, he began to tell me the story of why he had a box of broken violins. These were all rentals. Some even had tags hanging from them with the name and the year of the person that had rented the violin on one side and what was wrong with the violin on the other side.

Kyle told me it had been determined by the store owner that each of these violins was broken beyond repair, either literally or financially. He said the store owner was throwing them away. Kyle asked if he could have them rather than throwing them into the dump, and the store owner gave them to him. Just after his rather brief explanation, Kyle began to play and sing **"The Lord's Prayer"** on the first violin he had taken from the box. As he played and sang, tears formed in my eyes. Kyle was playing a violin that was obviously missing several pieces, including a part of the finger board and tuning pegs. It did not matter; the sound he produced was breathtaking.

Next, he picked out of the box a violin with no strings. Yes, that is correct; **there was not ONE string** on the violin. I was thinking, *How in the world is he going to play this one?* All of a sudden the instrument produced amazing, Godly, awe-inspiring music. I was so floored that I cannot even remember what song Kyle played and sang on the string-less violin. He used it like a drum or a bongo. The music was rich as he banged his fingers all over the front and back of the old, tattered, broken violin. About this time, I had a crowd gathering outside my office windows. Part of my staff had to see what was going on in my office.

Kyle picked up another violin. This one had a broken scroll and something rattled inside. Kyle explained that the rattle was the "sound post," an essential part of a violin – so essential that apparently there is a French name for this piece, meaning "the soul" of the violin. Kyle put the violin on his shoulder and began to play yet another song, **"Amazing Grace."** Trust me: even with "the soul" rattling around inside, the broken violin emitted a sound that took you right into the throne room of our Lord.

Kyle began to tell me that he almost took the box out of his car before he left his house to come see me. He had no intention of bringing the violins to our meeting, but he got busy and ran out of time. After hearing the Redento story, he understood it was a "God thing," leaving the box of broken violins in his car. Kyle went on to tell me that he had recently played a $16 million dollar violin, but the sound it made was no sweeter than the sound this bunch of tattered, torn, broken, dirty, and dusty violins had just made in my office. He was absolutely emphatic about it. Kyle said that even though the violins were broken and meant to be cast off by the store owner, **they still had souls.** They could still make beautiful music. They still needed to be played. No matter how broken they appeared on the outside, they still had music on the inside.

We live in a throw-away society today. We see little value in things that are used or broken. We just toss them to the curb and let the trash truck haul them off to the city dump. This is where these violins were headed before Kyle showed up to save them. The music Kyle played from them moved me and my staff to tears. My staff did not even realize Kyle was playing broken violins until after he had finished playing and singing. It was a good thing, too. If they had known, I think we might have had a mini-flood in the executive area of the bank that day.

As I told Kyle about my Redento, he connected my Redento Raffinato's meaning and story to his box of broken violins instantly.

Before he left my office, he gave me one of the broken violins from deep down in the bottom of the box. He dug around, looking for one that was the same size as the one my son Caleb had played many years ago. It was 1/16th the size of a full-size violin. Kyle found one and lifted it out of the box and handed it to me as a gift. I thanked him and immediately gave it back to him and kindly asked him to play a song on it too. It had a broken string and was missing several tuning pegs, a few of the fine tuners, too. He thumbed a string or two on it, adjusted the tune a bit, and played **"Alleluia"** on it. I wanted to start singing it with him. It was a moving rendition. I was so blessed that I am unable to describe my emotions of that moment adequately.

As Kyle left, I sat in my office and looked at my Redento and at the gift of my broken 1/16 violin sitting on my desk. I thought about what had just happened in my office. I noticed the violin had a tag on it, so I picked up the old violin and looked at the yellowish tag. It recorded that this violin started being used in 1976 as a rental. That was the same year my oldest son Jeremy was born. It was now 37 years old and rented out seven times, according to the tag. It would have been cast into the dump if Kyle had not saved it, just like the broken glass that was used to blow my Redento. I realized anew that God does not throw anything away. In fact, it is in the midst of our brokenness that we see Him for who He really is, the one and only true God who said, *"'I have loved you with an everlasting love; I have drawn you with unfailing kindness...'"* (Jeremiah 31:3).

What a great God I serve – we serve!

In the middle of our brokenness, when the world is sweeping us up, throwing us into a trash can and sending us to the dump for eternity, when the world no longer values what we offer, when the world has rejected us and thrown us away, **God can step in and breathe life back into our souls.** He can make us whole again. Listen to these words written by Robert Lowery in 1876: *"What can wash away my sin? Nothing but the blood of Jesus.* ***What can make me whole again?*** *Nothing but the blood of Jesus. This is all my hope and peace – nothing but the blood of Jesus. This is all my*

righteousness – nothing but the blood of Jesus. Now by this I'll overcome – nothing but the blood of Jesus. Now by this I'll reach my home – nothing but the blood of Jesus. Glory! Glory! This I sing – nothing but the blood of Jesus. All my praise for this I bring – nothing but the blood of Jesus."
Public Domain

Can you hear the violinist playing? **With God, nothing is wasted!**

Chapter 16

YOU CAN BE A REDENTO RAFFINATO

*"He gives strength to the weary
and increases the power of the weak."*
– Isaiah 40:29

Many, many Christians live life believing that once they accept Christ as their Savior, they will no longer have problems. They think becoming a Christian gives them the proverbial "get out of jail free card." Thinking like this is not Scriptural.

So many Christians are hurting or become disenchanted with their faith because they thought bad things would not happen to good people, and God's people are supposed to be good people. How can bad things happen to God's people? They seem to be saying that wearing the name of Jesus is some sort of insurance plan, alarm system, or suit of armor that protects one against pain. Unfortunately, this is not Scriptural.

The truth is that bad things do happen to Christians every day. Crummy, terrible, hurtful things happen to people that follow Jesus. Satan seeks to destroy, and he will load it on Christians, given the opportunity. Life loads it on everyone. **Christians are not immune to life.** Being a Christian does not insulate you from tragedy. In fact, here are just a few glimpses of significant problems some of my Christian friends are dealing with at this moment: One friend lost his job and has not been able to find steady work. Another friend had a horrible experience giving birth and now her only child appears to be destined to live life having to be totally cared for 24/7. Another friend's nine-year-old nephew was recently hit and killed by someone using a cell phone while driving.

I have more lousy stories about believers who are suffering. Obviously, being a Christian did not shelter them from a life of woeful events. I wish it did, but the truth is that **being a Christian does not give us immunity to life.**

Being a Christian *does* mean that we don't have to live a defeated life when heartache comes our way. It *does* mean that we have a God who loves us with an everlasting love and has promised to live with us every step of the way. It means He will not allow anything to come our way that He will not give us the power to overcome. Say, *"I am strong."* He loves you so much that He will help carry your load. *"'Come to me, all you who are weary and burdened, and I will give you rest...'"* (Matthew 11:28).

The power of Jesus living within a broken life is light to a darkened world. Jesus empowering us to live as salt and light while going through life's difficulties highlights the power of Jesus living within our souls. It is wonderfully attractive to a lost, hurting world. **It**

is the light in darkness. No amount of darkness, no amount of pain, can overcome the light. In fact, the opposite is true. **Darkness has no power over the light.**

Christians' hearts can become hardened towards God when they allow themselves to think that He caused terrible things to happen to them. The proper response is to seek God as a refuge in the midst of calamity. **He is there for us.** If we don't seek Him when life is lousy, we throw away a huge blessing. I met a guy last week who has been living a life filled with one bad thing after another, but get this: my new friend teasingly calls himself an overachiever because he has survived **four brain tumors!** He is a pastor – one of the good guys! But he is not safe from tumors. He has faced death squarely, eye to eye, toe to toe, four times. He could be mad at God. He could be swearing at God. He could be, but he is not. He has decided to live. He says, *"Maybe I have three months, three years, or thirty years; only God knows the day and time. I am going to live out my calling until He comes."* Now that is faith, that is trust, and that is **a guy who** *knows* **that God is the God of the broken.**

I have not been immune to brokenness. Years ago, I was broken by a series of life events. It was not my fault, but life dealt me some significant blows. I lost a job I loved very much. I lost a calling that I had been prepared to embrace. I was embarrassed. I was broke. In fact, I was so broke I had to work three jobs to provide for my family. One of the jobs was very public and humbling work, which made it hard to suck it up and go to work each day. Even with three jobs, we were struggling. One month, I had to sell my wedding ring to make a house payment. The next month, I had to sell an antique dining room table and chairs to make another house payment. Finally, I was forced to sell our home to protect my credit rating, only to rent the same house back from the guy who bought it from us. I was exhausted, I was humiliated, and I was financially broke. In fact, **I was plain broken**. In the middle of all of this, I had my third son, and **I named him Ezekiel.**

Why Ezekiel? Because of the 37th chapter of the book of Ezekiel, arguably the greatest Redento story ever. It is a story of a conversation between God and Ezekiel as they take a stroll in a valley. God takes Ezekiel to the Valley of Dry Bones. The Lord sets Ezekiel in the middle of a valley full of bones. Ezekiel's story goes like this:

"(2) He led me back and forth among them, and I saw a great many bones on the floor of the valley, bones that were very dry. (3) He asked me, 'Son of man, can these bones live?'

I said, 'Sovereign Lord, you alone know.'

(4) Then he said to me, 'Prophesy to these bones and say to them, 'Dry bones, hear the word of the Lord! (5) This is what the Sovereign Lord says to these bones: I will make breath enter you, and you will come to life. (6) I will attach tendons to you and make flesh come upon you and cover

you with skin; I will put breath in you, and you will come to life. Then you will know that I am the Lord.'

(7) So I prophesied as I was commanded. And as I was prophesying, there was a noise, a rattling sound, and the bones came together, bone to bone. (8) I looked, and tendons and flesh appeared on them and skin covered them, but there was no breath in them.

(9) Then he said to me, 'Prophesy to the breath; prophesy, son of man, and say to it, 'This is what the Sovereign Lord says: Come, breath, from the four winds and breathe into these slain, that they may live.' (10) So I prophesied as he commanded me, and breath entered them; they came to life and stood up on their feet—a vast army."

(Ezekiel 37:2-10)

These verses gave me so much hope. I looked to heaven, and I proclaimed Ezekiel 37 over my life and my family. As an act of faith, I named my third son after Ezekiel. It was a sign to the Lord and to my family, a constant reminder: **God is in control.** He can and will repair the brokenness in our lives if we allow Him to do so. My problems seemed small compared to the Valley of Dry Bones. **I knew that if God could breathe life back into those bones, he could redeem my life.** God made me into a **Redento Raffinato** in 1981.

Almost 15 years later, I failed God, my family and my friends. I thought I deserved to spend the rest of my life in the Valley of Dry Bones. I was humiliated, embarrassed and broken into many fragments; **my**

life was full of despair. I had ruined my kids' lives, destroyed my witness, and hurt my mom, brother, and sister-in-law. I hurt relatives on both sides of my family. **My days were dark.** They were long, and it seemed I was in the midst of a long drought that threatened my life and soul. But God was faithful. He sent someone to befriend me. He sent me to a foreign land where I met poverty, sickness, and despair like I had never known. In the midst of poverty and brokenness, my brokenness, I again met Jesus face to face. He welcomed me with open arms. He forgave me, He healed me, and He restored me.

You see, no matter what you have done, no matter where you are, no matter how many times you run from God, *He loves you with an everlasting love.* He is still on the throne. He forgives you, and He will redeem you. He never moves, He never stops calling, He never stops reaching His hand out to help you. No matter how scared you are, no matter how broken you are, **He forgives and restores.**

It is no accident you are reading this book right now. God's forgiveness is available to you today. His love, His presence, and His comfort can be yours. It is a free gift available to anyone and everyone. If you want to know Jesus, all you have to do is ask. Bow your head, and pray these words to the Lord:

"Lord Jesus, I am a sinner. I have broken so many rules; I have sinned against you. Jesus, today, forgive me, forgive my sins. Jesus, I want to live for you. I want to change. I

96

want to stop living in sin. Please forgive me. Please come into my heart today for eternity. I accept you as Lord of my life."

If you prayed the prayer, email me today at ross@rossalanhill.com and tell me. Then get to a Bible-believing church. Tell the pastor about your prayer and ask him to start helping you live your life for Jesus. Ask the pastor to explain baptism to you and ask him to baptize you.

Maybe you accepted the Lord some time ago and you have let life get between you and Jesus. You have allowed brokenness to creep in and separate you from Jesus. You are broken, possibly bitter, and you are separated from the Lord. Pray this prayer:
"Father, forgive me for not trusting you with my life. Forgive me for walking away from you, for trying to go through life on my own. Lord, today I turn my life back to you. Lord, heal my heart, restore me, and redeem me from my brokenness."

God is the God of the **Redento Raffinato**. He will remold you into something more beautiful than you can imagine. You can be a Redento Raffinato. Only through God can you become redeemed elegance.

AFTERWORD

Everyone needs to have a **"Spiritual Whatsit"** –
something like my Redento Raffinato or Kyle's
broken violins. What is your Whatsit? What could
you put in your office or home that would spark the
interest of your guests and provide you with an
opportunity to share the Lord?

Start looking for your Whatsit today. Your unique
item, that you can place in your office, home, or car,
that opens the door for you to share Jesus.

Put your imagination to work. Pray about it. Seek it
out.

Is it a painting? An antique book? Your
grandmother's Bible? A paper weight? A statue?

Maybe a Redento?

What is your "WHATSIT"?

Ross Alan Hill
building better lives

Ross Alan Hill is a man dedicated to building better lives. He has dedicated his life to helping people in all walks of life.

Hill has achieved success in business time and time again. He is known as a visionary in leading community banks. Hill is the founding President and CEO of Bank2 in Oklahoma City, Oklahoma. When he started Bank2 in 2002, it was the smallest bank in Oklahoma. Nationally, Bank2 is one of the top-rated community banks in the U.S. The *American Banking Journal* rated Bank2 as the number one community Bank in 2009 and number three in 2010. Bank2 has also won numerous awards including being named one of the Top 100 Native American Owned Businesses in America in each of the last 10 years and Bank2 was named one of Oklahoma's "Top Work Places for 2013."

Ross Alan Hill is also a much sought after international speaker. Over a recent thirteen month span Hill spoke forty seven times on five continents.

As a 35-year veteran banker, Hill has seen it all. This experience has given Hill a vision to take what he knows and work to change the world by helping people within business. Hill works with many businessmen and women, young college students, and entrepreneurs to help them structure strategic growth plans for their businesses. He loves to mentor and encourage them.

Historically, Hill has had the good fortune to work for The Federal Reserve Bank, Wells Fargo Bank, and Bank of Oklahoma. He has also founded a church and several other businesses and helped to establish some additional churches and non-profit ministries. Today, Hill serves as chairman of the board of Mission360 Foundation, Board of Directors for Giant Experiences, Business Advisory Board for Compassion International, and Board of Directors for the National Bankers Association.

Ross knows that 100% of his success is a gift from God. All praise is the Lord's.

Find Ross online at www.rossalanhill.com
Email: ross@rossalanhill.com
Facebook: www.facebook.com/rossalanhill
Twitter: @rossalanhill

Also join the journey at www.circle714.com

CPSIA information can be obtained
at www.ICGtesting.com
Printed in the USA
FFOW05n1605081116

9 780988 370067